CONTENT

CONTENTS

FOREWORD

Sadhu Sundar Singh, a contemporary of Mahatma Ghandi, was among the many Sikh converts to Christianity. He was also by far the holiest and most genuine.

His book *At the Feet of the Master*, first translated from Urdu by the Revd Arthur and Mrs Parker, was published in 1927. In the present edition Mrs Halcyon Backhouse, the editor, describes how Sundar Singh, disenchanted with the religion of his fathers, decided that he would put an end to his life if he could not discover the truth behind his agonising spiritual conflict. One morning he prayed until 4.30 a.m. and saw Jesus in a vision. From then on he became his disciple.

At the Feet of the Master is a record of the dialogues which took place between Jesus and his disciple and in which the mystery of faith was explored. Especially relevant today are the dialogues on the mystery of pain, suffering and sin, which so many aspiring Christians take exception to on the ground that a loving all-powerful God could not allow them to exist.

'Nothing among human beings,' wrote Simone Weil, 'has such power to keep our eyes fixed ever intensely on God than friendship for the friends of God.'

Sundar Singh was a friend of God. Let us be his friend, so that our eyes, too, may be fixed on God.

Kitty Muggeridge

INTRODUCTION

The Gurus, Swamis, Mahatmas and Sanyabi, whose poster images plaster the London Underground today, draw little concern from the Christian. But the Sadhu who rocked the West at the turn of this century still has the power to turn heads today.

India, perhaps most of all, has clearly demonstrated to the West man's thirst for God. In age after age the perpetual search goes on: the eternal quest is repeated. No one who has observed the East with its long line of pilgrims on their way to a sacred shrine can forget the mystery of this heart-longing to seek and find God's presence.

'Like as the hart desires the water brooks, so longs my soul for you, O God.' These words from Psalm 42 have a compulsive ring; in their beauty we see reflected that true man of God: the Sadhu.

When Sadhu Sundar Singh was a baby, his mother dedicated him to the life of religion. The word 'Sadhu', by which he became known both in the East and the West, means 'holy man'. It has a Hindu tradition behind it implying one who has chosen for himself the life of a homeless wanderer in search of spiritual truth. In India, throughout many centuries, men and women have left their homes, given up wealth and power, and set out in solitary faith on

this lonely search for God. Sundar Singh became
such a man. He was like the merchant in the Gospel
parable seeking the greatest pearls who, when he
had found the one pearl of great price, went and
sold all that he had and bought it. Sundar's heart
could not find its perfect rest until at last he
discovered in Christ himself the one pearl of great
price. Then the Sadhu sacrificed everything for it.

His Background

The Sikh religion was Sundar Singh's ancestral
religion. He was born of wealthy parents on
September 3rd, 1889, at Rampur, in the state of
Patiala in North India. Sundar was brought up in
the midst of luxury. He later often contrasted his
comfortable home and its soft ease made worthless
by spiritual disquiet, with a Sadhu's life, filled with
physical hardship, yet rich in the happiness of inner
joy and peace.

It was Sundar's mother who encouraged and
guided his unique religious leaning. When he was a
child she took him to priests and Sadhus to direct
his reading of the holy texts. By the age of seven he
knew by heart the *Bhagavadgita* of the Hindu
Scriptures. When his mother died he was fourteen
and the loss helped to increase his longing to find
God. The desire to obtain the inner peace to which
his mother had pointed grew deeply within him. By
sixteen he had read the *Granth* of the Sikhs, the
Muhammadan *Qur'an* and most of the Hindu
Upanishads – a remarkable achievement by any
standard. He had even practised Yoga to seek

identification with the Supreme Spirit. Sundar was proud to follow in the traditions of his Sikh heritage. He grew up repelled by the Christian religion which destroyed the religion of his forefathers.

His Conversion

In the two years that followed the death of his mother, the spiritual crisis welling up within Sundar came to a head. In the blank despair that seized him when his mother died, he found his religion powerless to help him. Each day he felt increasingly that he must find the truth which lay behind human existence. The ultimate questions of life and death had to be faced to the bitter end.

The blackness of despair turned to violence. At the age of fifteen Sundar took his mission school's copy of the Christian Gospels and set fire to it in public. Such extravagant rebellion against sacred books revealed a distraught mind. A wild resolve gripped him: either he would discover the truth behind his agonising spiritual conflict, or he would put an end to his own life. So he is quoted in his biography: 'I thought I had done a good deed by burning the Gospels, yet my unrest of heart increased. On the third day I could bear it no longer. I got up at three in the morning and prayed that if there was a God at all he would reveal himself to me' (*Sadhu Sundar Singh* by C F Andrews).

His intention was to place his head upon a railway line and kill himself if he got no answer. He prayed until 4.30 a.m. when he had a vision of the Lord

Jesus Christ. In a great light that looked like fire, the form of the Lord Jesus appeared in glory and love speaking to him in Hindustani: 'How long will you persecute me? I have come to save you; you were praying to know the right way. Why do you not take it?' Sundar Singh fell at the feet of his Saviour, filled with the peace he desperately sought. There he found heaven on earth.

Every detail of this tremendous experience burnt itself into the young man's mind. He never for a moment ever doubted its truth and reality. The abiding peace he felt that day never left him. 'I have had visions,' he later wrote, 'and I know how to distinguish them. But I have only seen Jesus once.' He distinguishes absolutely this conversion experience from all other visions which he frequently experienced later on through meditation and inner contemplation.

His Visions and Teachings

It is easy to question the mental balance of one who not only sees visions but takes them seriously. The lives of the mystics have always presented great difficulties to many who have no such experiences. Sadhu Sundar Singh never alluded to his visions in his public addresses; he only ever mentioned them, and then rarely, to his trusted friends.

The Sadhu's mind is an overflowing reservoir of anecdote, epigram and parable. He follows the tradition of Indian sages and poets: he thinks in pictures. He does not state a general principle and then buttress it with illustrations. He first puts the illustration and then draws out the general principle. His teaching is a complete theology in picture form. This Indian man who can live in total surrender to the will of Christ has little need of a Western systematic theology with all its arguments carefully worked out. He is no metaphysician, no scientist, no higher critic. His insight into moral and religious values is nearer to the New Testament writers than our modern world. His teaching is the spontaneous expression of prolonged meditation on the New Testament, and his simplicity of spiritual perception impresses all who hear his message.

His teaching has a peculiar freshness for a Western hearer. His words totally harmonise with his image of a saffron-robed turbaned Sadhu: they bear the marks of deep tranquillity. Here we have the words of a mystic of the twentieth century whose personality has attained inward unity.

The Sadhu's mysticism is centred in Christ. In this book we see a disciple with the lovelight beaming from his eyes. Seeing him one knows why a Christian has been defined as one, 'who has fallen in love with Christ'. This is the key to understanding his visions, his teaching, his whole way of life. In this book the Sadhu's spiritual perception unfolds in the form of a dialogue between himself, the disciple, and his Master, Jesus Christ.

His Work

The Sadhu is twice over a man who appeals to us today: a man in communion with the Divine and

impelled to a life of unselfish activity and practical
service to mankind.

The love of Christ urges the Sadhu to 'feed my
lambs'. That is why he became a missionary,
although his natural bent would have been towards
the hermit's life of contemplation in solitary
mountain caves. He did travel along those lonely
Himalayan mountains, but as a penniless Sadhu,
bringing relief to the poor and the message of Jesus
Christ to the needy.

The Sadhu's faith in Christ, won through agony
itself, meant for him a passing from death to life. To
declare to the world what had taken place, was
extremely painful. He had to explain the change of
religion and meet the opposition of his family and
friends. He had to bear the persecution meted out
to someone treated as insane. He was finally
thrown out of his luxurious home and driven from
his village. He spent his first homeless night cold,
hungry, thirsty, and without shelter or warm
clothes, sitting abandoned under a tree. But he
wrote, 'The presence of the Saviour changed the
suffering into peace.' On December 3rd, 1905, on
his sixteenth birthday, when in law he became an
adult, he was baptised.

The Sadhu's story describes the suffering of one
who seeks to make known the name of Jesus Christ.
It is a story of struggle against overwhelming odds,
coupled with joyous devotion to his Master that
never wavered.

His homeless condition as a wanderer, 'carrying
neither purse nor script', was thrust upon him by
his family and society. But Sundar gladly accepted it
for Christ's sake. It was a way of learning to be

Christ's true disciple. He made this choice: he would live his life as a wandering Sadhu, travelling without home or shelter from day to day. He preached the gospel in the Himalayan villages, meditating whenever he could find time. His ecstatic visions and deep meditations were the source of the physical strength he needed in this missionary work. He became the first Christian Sadhu – a revolutionary step for any young Indian Christian to take. He was determined to present Christ in an Indian form.

As a Sadhu, Sundar Singh was keeping to the ancient Indian tradition of abandoning all earthly ties in search of God. But as a Christian he added one supreme motive which transformed everything: the constraining love of Christ. It was this which supported him and gave him inward peace. He found the Yogin's peace and Bakhta's joy in the Lord Jesus.

Between the years of 1917 and 1929 Sadhu Sundar Singh travelled from the northern Himalayan regions of India and Tibet, to Burma, China, Japan, and then to England and other European countries, America and Australia, creating a new spiritual awakening in the places where he preached. He suffered hardships, persecutions and fiery trials.

Out of the Sadhu's home town of Rampur, through the river valley, the Hindustan-Tibet road rises quite abruptly. It reaches its higher levels by a very steep ascent. Thousands of feet below, the Sutley River disappears for a time and then reappears once more, tortuous amid the hills. This road soon trails off into nothing more than a very difficult and often dangerous mountain track, running along the high ledges that finally penetrate across the borders into Tibet. This long, narrow road deep into the North was the route the Sadhu walked on his missions to preach Christ to the Tibetans. With never failing courage Sadhu Sundar Singh journeyed many times along this road. Until once he never came back. After the mission of April 1929 he disappeared. Some time on that journey, probably in May or June, while seeking to reach Tibet, he entered into the presence of his Master. No one was by his side, but his Lord stood with him. Nobody can account for what happened. Nobody can trace his steps. His body was never found.

His soul sought union with God in solitude. But he died in love and service to his fellow men. His memory lives on. He has withstood the test of time so he can be truly called one of the great saints of our time.

NOTES ON THE TRANSLATION

At the Feet of the Master was written in Urdu in 1921 by Sadhu Sundar Singh. It was then translated by the Revd Arthur Parker and his wife Rebecca, both of whom were close friends of his. It was reprinted in English in 1922. The translators were able to work with the Sadhu to obtain a translation that preserved the true spirit and meaning of the original. For the Parkers, who had seen the Sadhu at work in India, it was not difficult to capture the atmosphere of his book. They had seen him, in true Oriental style, seated on the ground amid large crowds. They had observed the simplicity with which he laid bare a spiritual problem. In the introduction to their book, they speak of him as a man who, 'In his own gracious and dignified personality makes an indelible impression on the mind. He is more than a charming memory; he remains a compelling force in the lives of many who have sat with him at the Master's feet.'

Now I, in my turn, more than sixty years later, have above all tried to allow the Sadhu to speak to today's world. He speaks with all the quietude of spirit and deep understanding which pervade his words.

Halcyon Backhouse

LETTER FROM THE SADHU

'You call me "Teacher" and "Lord", and rightly so, for that is what I am' (John 13:13, NIV).

'Take my yoke upon you and learn from me, for I am gentle and humble in heart, and you will find rest for your souls' (Matt. 11:29, NIV).

There is nothing so perfect in the world as to be above objection and criticism. But the very sun which gives us light and warmth is not free from spots. Yet despite these defects it continues its regular duty. It is appropriate that we too should carry on to the best of our ability with what has been trusted to us; we must strive constantly to make our lives fruitful.

When the truths I have written about here were revealed to me by the Master they deeply affected my life. Some of them I have spoken of in my talks in Europe, America, Africa, Australia and Asia. Now, at the request of my friends, I have put them together in this little book. In setting it out like this, it is possible that defects will naturally occur. I am sure, however, that those who read this book with a prayerful and unprejudiced mind will be helped, just as I have been.

It is impossible to communicate the truths that have been revealed to me except in parabolic language. But by the use of such language my task has been made comparatively easy.

It is my prayer that God by his grace and mercy will bless you as he blessed me by these truths. So may they be a blessing to every one who reads them.

In humble service
Sundar Singh
June 30th, 1922

1 THE VISIONS

THE FIRST VISION

One dark night I went into the forest alone to pray. I sat upon a rock. There I laid before God my deep needs and begged his help. After a while I saw a poor man come towards me. I thought he was approaching me to beg some kind of relief because he was hungry and cold.

'I am a poor man, too,' I said to him. 'I have nothing at all but this blanket. You'd better go into the local village and get help there.' Then, as I was still in the middle of speaking, he flashed like lightning, showering drops of blessing, and disappeared immediately. What a bitter disappointment! It was clear to me, too late, that this had been my beloved Master. He came not to beg from a poor wretch like me, but to bless and enrich me (2 Cor. 8:9). I remained there weeping. With what sorrow I regretted my utter stupidity and lack of insight!

THE SECOND VISION

I went back to the forest to pray another day, after I had finished my work. As I sat on the same rock I thought about what blessings to pray for. While I

was doing this it seemed as though another person
came and stood near me. From his bearing and dress
and way of speaking, he seemed to me to be a well
respected and devoted servant of God, yet his eyes
glittered with deceit and cunning. As he spoke it
was as if he breathed an odour of hell. He said to me:

Holy and honoured sir, pardon me for interrupt-
ing your prayers and breaking in on your privacy.
But it is one's duty to try to promote the welfare
of others, so I have come to lay an important
matter before you. Your pure unselfish life has
made a deep impression not only on me but on a
great number of devout people. In God's name
you have sacrificed yourself body and soul for
others, but have you been truly appreciated?
What I mean is, as a Christian you have
influenced only a few thousand other Christians,
some of whom even distrust you. Wouldn't it be
much more worth while if you became a Hindu or
a Mussulman? Then you could really become a
great leader. They are looking for such a spiritual
leader. Consider what I'm suggesting; if you
accept it, then three hundred and ten million
Hindus and Muslims will become your followers.
And pay you enormous respect and honour.

As soon as I heard this these words rushed from
my lips:

You Satan! Get out! I knew you immediately.
You're the wolf in sheep's clothes! Your single
desire is for me to renounce the cross and the
narrow path that leads to life, and to choose the

broad road of death. My Master himself is my lot and my life. He gave himself, his very life, for me and so it is right that I should offer my own life to him as a sacrifice, for he is everything to me. Get away! I have nothing to do with you.

On hearing my reply the deceiver went off grumbling and growling in rage. I, in my tears, poured out my soul to God in prayer:

My Lord God, you who are everything to me, life of my life, spirit of my spirit, look on me in mercy, so fill me with your Holy Spirit that my heart shall have no room for love of anything else but you alone. I seek from you no other gift but that of yourself, the giver of life with all its blessings. From you I ask not for the world or its treasures. But you alone I desire and long for; where you are there is heaven. My heart hungers and thirsts; it can only be satisfied by you who gave it birth. O my Creator, you have formed my heart for yourself alone and no other. It can find no rest or ease except in you, my Creator, who has placed in my heart this longing for rest. Remove then from me all that is opposed to you and come into my heart to stay and rule for ever. Amen.

When I rose from this prayer I half-saw through my tears, a glowing being dressed in light and beauty, standing before me. Though he did not speak a word yet there poured from him lightning-like rays of life-giving love, the power of which penetrated and bathed my very soul. At once I knew that my dear Saviour stood before me. Immediately

I arose from my seat upon the rock and fell at his feet. He held in his hand the key of my heart. Opening its innermost chamber with his key of love, he filled me with his presence, and whenever I looked within or outside myself I saw only him.

At that moment, I knew that man's heart is the very throne and fortress of God; that when he enters there to take up residence heaven begins.

In those few seconds he so filled my heart and spoke such wonderful words that I could not tell them all, no matter how many books I wrote. For the things of heaven can be spoken of only in heavenly language; earthly tongues are not sufficient for them.

Yet I will try to write of some of those things of heaven which came to me from the Master by this means of vision. Upon the very rock where I had just sat, the Master seated himself. With me at his feet there flowed between us, Master and disciple, the following conversation.

2 THE MANIFESTATION OF GOD'S PRESENCE

DIALOGUE I

The disciple:

O Master! Fountain of life! Why do you hide yourself from those who adore you and do not delight the eyes of those who long to gaze upon you?

The Master:

1. My true child, true happiness does not depend upon physical sight. It comes through spiritual vision and depends upon the heart. In Palestine thousands looked at me, but that did not give them all true happiness. Mortal eyes perceive those things which are mortal; physical eyes cannot see the immortal God or spiritual beings. You yourself cannot see your own spirit, so how can you look at its Creator? However, when your spiritual eyes are opened then most certainly you can see God who is Spirit (John 4:24). What you now see of me is not seen with your physical eyes but with the eyes of the spirit.

When thousands of people saw me in Palestine, did they all see me with their spiritual eyes opened, or did I myself become mortal? Not at all! I took on a mortal body in order to give a ransom for the sins of the world. When the work of salvation for sinners was completed (John 19:30), then what was immortal transformed what was mortal into glory. So after the resurrection only those who had received spiritual sight were able to see me (Acts 10:40-1).

2. There are many people in this world who know *about* me but do not *know* me. Since they have no personal relationship with me, they have no understanding of me, or faith in me, and do not accept me as their Saviour and Lord.

It is like talking about reds, blues and yellows with a man born blind. He remains totally unaware of their beauty and charm. They mean nothing to him. He knows about them, he knows their names, but he lacks a true appreciation of their colour. That he can only know if his eyes are opened. Similarly, until a man's spiritual eyes are opened he cannot *know* me. However scholarly he may be he cannot see my glory, my divine nature; he cannot understand that I am God incarnate.

3. Then there are many believers who are aware of my presence in their hearts, bringing them spiritual life and peace, who cannot clearly see me. In the same way, the human eye cannot at first see properly when medicine has been dropped into it, but it feels the presence of the medicine, cleansing deep into the eye, and promoting the power of sight.

The true peace born by my presence in the hearts

of believers is not visible, but they can feel its power and are happy in it. Nor can they see the happiness of mind and heart that is theirs as they enjoy the peace of my presence.

4. The same analogy can be made using the sense of taste. The tongue tastes sweetness, but sweetness remains invisible. In the same way, I give my children life and joy with the hidden manna, that bread of which the world with all its knowledge does not and never can know (Rev. 2:7).

Sometimes during sickness the sense of taste is impaired, and however delicious the food given to the sick person may be, it tastes unpleasant to him. In the same way sin distorts one's spiritual taste so that word and service and presence lose their attraction to the sinner. Instead of benefiting from them he starts to argue about them and criticise them.

5. In addition, many believers (like the man born blind who received back his sight) are able to see Jesus as a prophet and as the Son of Man, but do not regard him as the Christ, the Son of God (John 9:35-7), until I am revealed to them a second time in power.

6. A mother once hid in a garden, among some thick shrubs. Her little son was hunting for her and crying as he searched. He looked high and low through the whole garden but could not find his mother. A servant came to him, 'Sonny, don't cry! Look at the mangoes on this tree. And look at the pretty flowers. Come on, I'll get some for you.' But the child cried out, 'No! No! I want my mother. The food she gives me is nicer than all these mangoes and her love is sweeter than all these flowers. This

garden is mine, anyway, because all that my mother has is mine. No! I want my mother.'

When the mother, hidden in the bushes, heard this she rushed out and caught her child to her breast, smothering him with her love and kisses. That garden became paradise to the child. In the same way, too, my children cannot find any true joy in this great garden of the world, though it is so full of charming and beautiful things, until they find me. I am their Emmanuel who is ever with them. I make myself known to them (John 14:21).

7. Just as the sponge lies in the water and the water fills the sponge, but the water is not the sponge and the sponge is not the water, but they remain different, so my children abide in me and I in them. This is not pantheism. This is the kingdom of God which belongs to my children in this world. And just as the water fills the sponge, so I am in every place and in everything, but my identity is not lost (Luke 17:21).

Wash a piece of charcoal and its blackness will not disappear, but let the fire enter into it and its dark colour vanishes. So, too, when the sinner receives the Holy Spirit (who is from the Father and myself for we are both one) it is the baptism of fire. In it all the blackness of sin is driven away and that sinner is made a light to the world (Matt. 3:11-14). Like the fire in the charcoal, I abide in my children and they in me, and through them I make myself known to the world.

DIALOGUE 2

The disciple:

Master, if you made a special manifestation of yourself to the world, men would no longer doubt the existence of God and your own divine nature. They would all believe and enter upon the way of holiness.

The Master:

1. My son, I know every man's inner state. I know well and I reveal myself to each heart, according to its needs. There is no better way of bringing man into holiness than by revealing myself to him. I became man, so that men may know God. I came to reveal that God is not as a distant stranger or a tyrant, but one full of love and no stranger to man, for man was made in the image of God.

Man has this natural desire to see the God whom he loves. But the Father cannot be seen. God is by nature incomprehensible. He who would comprehend God must have his nature. Man is a comprehensible creature and as such he cannot see God. Yet God is love and he has endowed man with that same faculty of love. So in order that man's craving for love might be satisfied, God adopted a form of existence that man could comprehend. And God became man. He is visible to his children. They may see him and enjoy him with all the holy angels (Col. 1:15; 2:9). That is why I said, 'Anyone who has seen me has seen the Father' (John 14:9–10, NIV).

And although I am called the Son, while I am in the form of man, I am the eternal and everlasting Father (Isa. 9:6).

2. I and the Father and the Holy Spirit are one. In the sun there is both heat and light, but light is not heat and heat is not light, yet both are one, though different in their forms. Similarly, I and the Holy Spirit, proceeding from the Father, bring light and heat into the world. The Spirit which is the baptismal fire, burns to ashes all sin in the hearts of believers making them pure and holy. I, who am the true Light (John 1:9; 8:12), disperse all dark, evil desires and lead believers in the way of holiness, to bring them finally to their eternal home. Yet we are not three but one, just as the sun is one.

3. Whatever worth and power and ability God has given to man must be put to use, otherwise it gradually decays and dies. So faith, if it is not truly fixed on the living God, is shattered by the shock of sin and it turns to doubt. It is often said, 'If only this or that doubt could be removed then I'd be ready to believe.' That is like asking the doctor to remove the pain before setting the broken limb, which is silly, because the pain comes from the broken limb and when that is set the pain will stop. So man's tie with God has been snapped by sin, and doubts – which are the spiritual pains – have arisen. What is needed is for union with God to be renewed again, and then those doubts about my divine nature and the existence of God will automatically disappear. In place of pain will flow that wonderful peace which the world cannot give or remove. This is why I became flesh: that broken men may be reunited with God and that they may be happy with him in

heaven for evermore.

4. God is love. He has given this ability to love to all living creatures, and especially to man. And it is only right that the lover who has given his life and love should receive our tribute of love – which is his due. God loves all his creation and if the love he gives us is not used properly then it turns to selfishness. If we do not love God with all our heart, soul, and strength, with the love he has put within us, then our love falls from its high calling and becomes self-centred. So disaster rises within the world for man and all God's creatures. In a strange way, every selfish person is a self-destroyer.

I have also said, 'Love your neighbour as yourself.' This refers, of course, to all men, since in one sense all men are neighbours. However, it especially includes those who constantly live near to each other. It is easy to live at peace with a fellow neighbour just for a few days, even if he is unfriendly to you. But to show constant love when he is persistently troubling to you, is extremely difficult. In times like these you must love him as yourself.

When within one's own community one has won the battle to love at all times, then it becomes easier to love all others as yourself. When a man loves God with all his heart, mind and soul, and his neighbour as himself, then doubts disappear. In that man, God's kingdom will be established for ever. Melted and moulded in the fire of love that man will be restored into the likeness of the heavenly Father who in the beginning made man in his own image.

5. I manifest myself through my word to those who seek me with a pure heart. Just as I took on a human

body for man's salvation, so my word, which is Spirit and life (John 6:63), is written in the language of men. Both inspired and human elements are united in it. And just as men do not understand me, they do not understand my word. It is not necessary to know Hebrew and Greek in order to understand it – what is needed is the fellowship of the Holy Spirit. It is this abiding in the Holy Spirit of which the prophets and apostles wrote. Without a doubt the language of my word is spiritual and only the person born of the Spirit is able to understand it fully. It does not matter whether that person knows all the world's critical arguments, or is just a child, the language of the Spirit is understood by the person in the Spirit; it is his mother tongue. So remember this: The wisdom of the world cannot understand it for they have no share in the Holy Spirit.

6. I, the author of the book of nature, freely manifest myself in creation. To read this book and find me there, men also need spiritual insight, otherwise they will go wrong.

The blind man uses the tips of his fingers as eyes and can read a book. But he cannot assess the truth he reads simply by touch. He must use his understanding. The agnostics and sceptics who investigate truth and find only defects instead of perfection are a case in point. Fault-finding critics ask, 'If there is an almighty Creator of the world why are there defects in it? Why do we have natural disasters, pain, suffering, death?' Their error is similar to the mistake made by the ignorant man who finds fault with an unfinished work of art. When he sees the complete picture, he feels a sense of shame and ends up singing the praises of its author. God did not form the world as it now is in one day, nor will it reach perfection in one day. The whole of creation moves forward to perfection. If we of this world could look from God's perspective, and see the perfect world that it will one day be, then we too will say, in praise, all is very good (Gen. 1:31).

7. The human spirit lives in the body, rather like the chicken in its shell. If one told the chicken of the great outside world which it would see when it was set free of its shell, the chicken would not understand or believe it. If one told it that its feathers and eyes would enable it to see and fly, it would not believe it. And there would be no way of proving it to the unborn chick until it came out of its shell.

So in the same way many are uncertain about life after death and the existence of God, because they cannot see beyond the shell-like body of flesh. Their thoughts, like feeble wings hampered by the shell, cannot take flight beyond the narrow confines of the brain. Their weak eyes cannot discover those eternal unfading treasures which God has prepared for those who love him (Isa. 64:4; 65:17). The conditions necessary for attaining eternal life are like those of the chicken egg which is hatched by the warmth of the mother hen. If we are to receive eternal life, we should receive in faith the life-giving warmth of the Holy Spirit.

8. There are many who say that a beginning must have an end. This is not true. God who is able, at his will, to bring into being something from nothing is also able by his powerful word to confer immort-

ality upon what he has made. If this were not so he could not be called Almighty God. Life in this world decays and is destroyed because it is subject to those things which are themselves subject to change and decay. But if this life were set free from those influences of death it would attain eternity. By being brought under the care of the eternal unchanging God, who is the fountain and source of life, it will escape death's clutch.

For those who believe in me, 'I give them eternal life, and they shall never perish; no one can snatch them out of my hand' (John 10:28, NIV), 'I am the Lord God almighty that is, was and will be' (Rev. 1:8).

3 SIN AND SALVATION

DIALOGUE 1

The disciple:

Master, it is clear to almost everyone that disobedience to God and refusal to worship him is sin. The deadly result of this state of affairs is evident in the world. But the exact nature of sin we are not clear about. How, in almighty God's very presence, in opposition to his will, and in his own world, did sin come to be?

The Master:

1. Sin is to live according to one's own will and cast aside the will of God. It is to dispense with God's truth and law and to satisfy one's own desires. In so doing, one thinks one can possess real happiness. Sin has no individuality – no one can say that someone has created it. Sin is simply the name given to a state or condition. There is only one Creator God and he is good. He could not have created a bad thing because that would mean he acted contrary to his own nature. Apart from the one Creator there is no other who could have created sin. Satan can spoil what God has created,

but he has no power to create anything. Sin, then, is not a part of God's creation, nor is it a self-created existence. It has no individuality or personality, but is simply a delusive, destructive state of non-being.

Here is an example: light possesses real existence but darkness does not. Darkness exists only as a state in the absence of light. Sin or evil, then, is not a self-existent thing, but merely the absence or non-existence of good. This dark state of evil is most horrific. Because of it many miss the right course and are shipwrecked on the rock of Satan. There they fall into the darkness of evil and are lost in hell. For this reason I, the light of the world, was revealed as a man. I came to rescue those who put their trust in me from the power of darkness, and bring them safely home to heaven, where there is neither name nor sign of darkness (Rev. 21: 23; 22:5).

2. You ask how this dark state of sin came to be in the very presence of the Lord of creation? It arose because Satan and men wilfully sought to carry out their own desires and live in an unlawful, wrong way. But yet, you ask, why did God not create man in such a way that he could not fall into this evil state? The answer is that man would then have had to be constructed like a machine, without free will or choice. To enter the state of true happiness in God, one must act from within one's own free choice.

Adam and Eve fell prey to the beguiling tricks and deceit of Satan. In their sinless state they had not known there were such things as lies and deceit. Before that Satan himself had not known of the existence of the pride for which he was cast out of heaven, because no such thing as pride had previously existed. Yet although this state of sin in both men and Satan came into God's world, God has by his almighty power given that state another dimension by bringing good out of its evil.

First, God's boundless love has been revealed. It has taken form in the birth of Jesus and he has redeemed the world. This would not have happened in different circumstances and would have remained a hidden mystery of God. Second, the redeemed, having tasted the bitterness of sin, will all the more richly enjoy the happiness of heaven, just as after a bitter taste the sweetness of honey gives greater delight. In heaven the redeemed sin no more, but serve their Father God in meekness and obedient love, abiding in him in joy for evermore.

3. Men are keen to discover faults – such as spots or eclipses – in the sun and moon. But they give no thought to the dark spots and eclipses of sin. You can measure from their attitude to sin how great the darkness is in men. The very light they have is darkness (Matt. 6:23). Sin has deadened man's heart and mind so that they have no sense of disgust or pain, just as the body of the leper becomes numb to pain. But the time will come when man will awake to the terrible ravages of sin, and then there will be weeping and gnashing of teeth.

4. There are many immersed in sin who are unaware of its weight, like the man who dives into the water unaware of its ton weight until he is drowned by it. The man who emerges from the water and tries to carry some away with him soon realises just how heavy even a little bit of water is.

Anyone who knows the burden of sin and comes to
me in penitence freely receives rest, for it is such
people that I came to seek and to save (Matt. 11:28;
Luke 19:10).

5. Before death occurs it is not necessary for every
single member of the body to become useless and
weak. A weakness or injury to the heart or brain is
enough to bring life to an end despite the health and
strength of the rest of the body. In the same way by
its poisonous effect on the mind and heart one sin is
sufficient to ruin the spiritual life not just of that
one person, but of a whole family, a nation, even a
whole race. Such was the sin of Adam. Yet, just as
one word from me could raise Lazarus from death
to life, so I am sufficient to give eternal life to all.

6. Sometimes it happens that an animal or bird stays
for a long while with man and then returns to its
own kind. But they, instead of welcoming it, set
upon it and kill it. The reason for this is that its long
familiarity with man has changed the bird, and its
habits are not the same as those of the other birds.
Similarly animals reject from their society those of
their kind who have come under the influence of
man. So how can saints and angels in heaven live
with those who have lived closely with wicked
men? This does not mean that saints and angels
have no love for sinful men, but that the pure life of
heaven will itself be distasteful to such men. For
clearly, when sinners dislike the company of good
men in this world, how can they be happy in their
company throughout eternity? To them heaven
would be as distasteful as hell itself!

Don't suppose that God will turn sinners out of
heaven and cast them into hell because he wants to.

God would never cast anyone into hell. It is the sinner's foul life that makes him throw himself into hell. Within each man's heart is his own heaven or hell. It exists now, long before the end of life when heaven and hell draw near, and it is measured according to the good or evil nature of each man. So anyone who longs to be saved from that eternal torment, must truly repent of his sins and give his heart to me. By me and through the power of the Holy Spirit a man may become, for ever, a child of the kingdom of God.

7. A rebel against a king or government in this world may save himself by taking refuge in another country. But where shall a rebel against God flee for safety? Wherever he goes, even to heaven or hell, he will find God ever present (Ps. 139:7–8). He will find his safety only in repentance and submission to his Lord.

8. The fig leaves were too scanty a covering for Adam and Eve, so God gave them coats of skin. And before God's anger man's good deeds are as useless as fig leaves. Nothing will save man from God's anger but my robe of righteousness.

9. The moth does not think of the burning and destructive power of the flame, but rushes into it, fascinated by its brilliance, and dies. Man, too, rushes into his eternal destruction, lured into sin, thoughtless of its destructive, poisonous power. But my light saves the sinner from death. It gives life and enduring happiness. Man was capable of accepting the precious gift of my true light.

10. Sin is not an illusion or a figment of the imagination. In the state of spiritual darkness where the evil will of man is exercised, living seeds

have come into existence containing such evil that they have infected his spirit for ever and will finally destroy it, just as smallpox can destroy the beauty of man, turning him into repulsive ugliness. God did not create evil, and he did not create disease and bodily pains. They are quite simply the natural result of man's disobedience. Pain and disease are not things of the imagination. They are the visible expression of the unseen disease of sin. And this sin may be personal or that of someone else in the family of man. When all the members of the family repent and are united to me my health-giving blood circulates through all. It heals all their internal hidden diseases and gives them eternal health. It was for such a healthy state that man was created, that he might dwell ever with his Lord and Master in happiness.

DIALOGUE 2

The disciple:

Master, today some scholars and their followers say that you were a great teacher and example for man's spiritual life, but that salvation and eternal happiness depend on one's own efforts and good deeds. So they make your atonement and redemption meaningless and futile.

The Master:

1. Don't ever forget that spiritual and religious ideas connect with the heart more than the head. The heart is the temple of God and when it is filled with God's presence then the head is enlightened. The mind and eye of understanding are useless without the true light, just as natural eyes are sightless without daylight. In the dark one may mistake a rope for a snake. The worldly-wise pervert spiritual truth and lead simple minds astray. Satan beguiled Eve with the most crafty of all the animals, the serpent, not the sheep or the dove. So he takes the wisdom and the skill of the wise and uses them as instruments suited to his own purpose. It is not enough to be learned and clever. It is the innocence of the dove that I required when I said, 'Be wise as serpents, harmless as doves' (Matt. 10:16).

2. My cross and atonement do for believers what the serpent of brass did for the Israelites. In the wilderness the brass serpent saved the men who looked up at it in faith (Num. 21:9; John 3:14–15), though some did not believe but were critical. They said:

> If Moses had prescribed a powerful drug as an antidote for the poisonous snakes that would have provided a good reason to exercise faith. But what power can a pole have over this venom? Those with such an attitude died. Today too those who object to the method of salvation which God has appointed will perish in the poison of their own sin.

3. A young man fell down a precipice. When rescuers reached him he was so badly injured and had lost so much blood that he was at the point of death. His father took him to the doctor who said, 'This man has lost too much blood. If anyone is prepared to give his own blood he may recover, otherwise he will die.' The father, whose heart overflowed with love for his son, offered his own blood and the son lived.

Man has fallen from the mount of holiness and lies broken and wounded by his sins. Through those wounds his spiritual life has ebbed away and he is near to death. But I pour out my own eternal spiritual blood for those who believe in me so that they may be saved from death and gain eternal life. This is the purpose of my coming. It is so that they may have life, full to overflowing, and live in eternity (John 10:10).

4. In times of old, men would not eat certain foods, or drink the blood of animals, in the belief that this would keep them from certain diseases and also would not encourage or strengthen the animal nature within them. But now, 'My flesh is real food and my blood is real drink' (John 6:55). By my body and blood man can receive perfect health and heavenly joy and happiness.

5. You don't get full salvation just because your sins have been forgiven. Full salvation only comes when you are set completely free from all sin. It is possible for a man to receive full pardon for his sins and yet die from the disease of his sin. For example, a man was ill for some time and as a result his brain was affected. In this state he attacked and killed another man. The death sentence was repealed when his

relatives explained the circumstances in which it had happened. The man was granted a pardon for the crime of murder. But before his friends could reach him with the good news, indeed as they were on their way, the man died of the very illness which had caused the murder.

Now what advantage was this pardon to the murderer? Had his disease been cured the man would have been safe and then his pardon would have given him true happiness.

This is why I was revealed in the flesh: to save penitent believers from the disease of sin, from its punishment and from death. I came to remove both the cause of sin and its results. They will not die in their sins, for I will save them (Matt. 1:21). They shall pass from death to become heirs of eternal life.
6. For many people life is packed with dangers. They are like the hunter who caught sight of a honeycomb on a branch overhanging a stream. He climbed up the tree and began to enjoy the honey. He was quite unaware of the danger he was in – that below him an alligator lay with open jaws waiting for him to fall into the stream; that a pack of wolves had gathered round the foot of the tree eager for the hunter to descend; and that worst of all, the tree itself was rotten, eaten away by insects and ready to fall. In due course, the unwary hunter fell straight into the jaws of the alligator.

It is like this for the human spirit who enjoys for a short time the attractive and fleeting pleasure of sin. Ensconced in the body, it gathers in the honeycomb. It has no idea that it lies in the midst of a fearsome jungle where Satan crouches ready to tear the human spirit to pieces, and hell waits open-mouthed like the alligator, poised to gulp it down, while worst of all the tiny insects of sin have eaten away the very roots and life of the man. Soon the soul falls and becomes the prey of hell.

But the sinner who comes to me I will deliver from sin, from Satan and from hell. I will give him eternal joy, which no one will take away from him (John 16:22).

7. Satan draws men to himself with crafty, enticing words, and then swallows them down just as a snake fascinates little birds with its glittering eye and swallows them. But those who believe in me I deliver from that old serpent and from all the soul-destroying attractions of this world. I will set them as free as birds to fly freely through the open heaven. Resisting the force of earth's gravity, they will mount on wings of prayer and reach home safe at last, their hearts drawn by the sweetness of my love.

8. Just as everything seems yellow to a man with jaundice, so to the sinner truth is moulded to the shape of his sin. And it comes as no surprise when such people go one step farther and put me down as a sinner like themselves. But my work, which is to save sinners, does not depend on the good opinion of the world. It continues to move undisturbed in the lives of believers. Just as Levi paid tithes to me when he was still unborn in Abraham's loins, so through my death on the cross all generations of believers have in me the atonement and ransom for their sins, though they were not at that time even born. For my salvation is for all races of men in the world.

9. It is rubbish to say that a man can get hold of

salvation by his own efforts and by good works without being born again. Rulers and teachers of ethics say, 'Become good by doing good.'

But this is what I say, 'Become good yourself before doing good works.'

When that new, good life becomes yours, then good deeds will be the natural result.

Only a fool says that a bitter tree will finally become sweet by constantly bearing fruit. A bitter tree can only become sweet by being grafted on to a sweet tree. The goodness of the sweet tree passes into the bitter one and it is gradually changed. This is what we call a new creation.

The sinner may want to do what is right, yet it will only result in sin. But when he repents and is grafted into me by faith, the old nature in him dies and he becomes a new person. Then from this new life, whose origin lies in my salvation, good deeds spring as the fruit and they abide for ever.

10. There are many who have learnt from experience that man's natural goodness cannot bring true peace of heart. Neither can it make him certain of salvation or of eternal life. This was true of the young man who came to me seeking eternal life. His thoughts about me were wrongly conceived from the beginning, just as many worldly-wise men today have a misconception of who I am. That young man assumed I was like one of those teachers who are white-washed sepulchres, in whose lives there is not an atom of goodness. That's why I said to him, 'Why do you ask me about goodness? There is no one good but One.' But he failed to see in me the One who gives goodness and life. When I tried to draw him into my friendship, to

make him a truly good man and to grant him life, the young man became sad and left me. Yet his life clearly shows that he was not satisfied with keeping the commandments and that his own goodness did not bring him the certainty of eternal life. He would not have come to me if his good works had given him peace, nor would he have left me in sorrow (Mark 10:17–23).

Now long afterwards another young man, Paul, recognised me and the desire of his heart was completely filled. He did not turn away in sadness but gave up all that he had and followed me (Phil. 3:6–15). So everyone who stops trusting in his own self-righteousness and follows me, will receive eternal life from me and true peace.

4 PRAYER

DIALOGUE 1

The disciple:

I have sometimes heard people ask, 'Since God is fully aware of our needs and knows how to supply them in the best way, whether we are good or evil, why should we pray to him about them? Can our prayers – for any of our needs – actually alter the will of God?'

The Master:

1. Those who ask such a question show clearly that they do not know what prayer is. They have not lived a life of prayer or they would know that prayer is not a form of begging to God. Prayer is an effort to lay hold of God himself, the author of life. When we have found him, the source of life, and have entered into communion with him, then the whole of life is ours. With God we have all that will make life perfect.

God gives evil-doers what they need for their life in this world because he loves them. But he does not even show them their spiritual needs because they

have no spiritual life. If God were to shower them
with his spiritual blessings they would not appreciate them, but to believers God gives all kinds of
gifts, especially his spiritual blessings, with the
result that very soon they scarcely notice earthly
blessings, fixing their love on the unseen and
spiritual.

You cannot *alter* the will of God, but the man of
prayer can discover God's will. For such men who
pray God reveals himself in the hidden chamber of
the heart and there he speaks with them. When
God shows them that his loving plans and actions
are for their good, then their doubts and difficulties
pass away for ever.

2. Prayer is a breathing in of the Holy Spirit. God so
pours his Holy Spirit into the life of the prayerful
that they become 'living souls' (Gen. 2:7; John
20:22). They will never die. The Holy Spirit pours
himself into their spiritual lungs through prayer,
filling them with health, power and eternal life.

God is love and he freely gives what is necessary
for both the earthly and spiritual life. He offers
salvation and his Holy Spirit to everyone just as
freely, but people treat them casually. It is prayer
that teaches us to value them. They are as
necessary as air and water, heat and light, without
which life is impossible. God has freely provided all
that is necessary for the spiritual life. But men put
so little value on these things that they don't thank
God for them. Yet men will greatly value God's
gifts of gold and silver and precious stones which
are gained with great difficulty and are rare, even
though the hunger and thirst of the body and the
longings of the heart cannot be satisfied by them.

This is the sort of stupidity that men of this world display in regard to spiritual things, but to the man of prayer God gives true wisdom and eternal life.

3. This world is like a huge ocean in which men sink and drown. Yet marine animals can carry on their life in the deepest water because they come up to the surface and take in air. So they can live in the depths. And so too those who rise to the surface of this life's ocean and in prayer, breathe in the life-giving Spirit of God, those people find life and safety even in this world.

4. Although fish spend their whole life in the sea's salt water, they don't themselves become full of salt. They still live. Similarly, the man of prayer remains free of the sinful taint of this sin-defiled world in which he lives because he keeps his life through prayer.

5. Water from the sea is drawn upwards by the hot rays of the sun and all bitterness and salt are left behind. Gradually this sweet, refreshing water forms clouds which fall in showers on the earth. That is how it is when the thoughts and desires of the man of prayer rise up like misty emanations of the soul, the rays of the sun of righteousness purify them from sin and his prayers become great clouds from heaven bursting into showers of blessing, refreshing many on earth.

6. The waterfowl spends its life swimming in the water yet when in flight its feathers are perfectly dry. So with men of prayer – when they rise high above this sin-polluted world to go to their eternal home they arrive free from any spot or stain of sin.

7. A ship is made to be in water, yet it is dangerous for water to flow into the ship. So a man has his life

in this world – and that's good. As he keeps himself
afloat and he can help others, together they enable
each other to sail to life's harbour. But if the world
seeps through into his heart it means death and
destruction and he will sink. So the man of prayer
always reserves his heart for Jesus who formed it to
be his temple. In this way he rests in peace and
safety now in this world, and in the world to come.
8. We all know that without water it is impossible to
live; yet if we sink under it, we die. We need water,
but we mustn't drown in it. So the world and
worldly things must be used wisely: without them
life is impossible. God created the world for men to
use and enjoy. But man must not drown himself in
it. To sink into the world means that the breath of
prayer is stopped and man will die.
9. If man stops living by prayer, the life of the Spirit
begins to fail. Worldly things which were intended
to be useful then become hurtful and destructive.
By its heat and light the sun causes all vegetation to
flourish, but it also makes it shrivel and die. The air
gives life and vigour to living beings, yet it is the air
that makes them go rotten. So man must 'watch
and pray', and use the things of this world wisely
and to his spiritual advantage.
10. We must live in this world as people who are in it
but who do not belong to it. Then the things of this
world will help us grow in the spiritual life instead
of hurting and destroying it. The condition for all
spiritual growth is that a man keeps his face turned
towards the sun of righteousness.
11. It sometimes happens that in a plot of dirty,
filthy ground flowers spring up and flourish, and
the sweet scent of the flowers overpowers the evil

smell. The plants have turned towards the sun and received its light and heat, and the filth, instead of being hurtful to them, fertilises them, helping them to grow and flourish. So the man of prayer who turns his heart to me receives my light and warmth and the sweet scent of his new holy life glorifies me amid the smell of this evil world. From such a man rises not only sweet scents but fruit which lasts for ever.

DIALOGUE 2

1. Praying does not imply that without prayer God does not give us anything, nor that God is unaware of our needs until we pray. But praying has this great advantage: the soul is best fitted to receive God himself, as well as his blessings, when it is in an attitude of prayer. It was not after one but after ten days of special preparation that the apostles were able to receive the outpouring of the fullness of the Spirit.

If a blessing were given to one who was not ready to receive it, he would not value it sufficiently nor be able to keep it for very long. There is the example of Saul who received the Holy Spirit and the kingship without seeking for them. Very soon he lost them both. Saul had not set out from home to seek God and his Holy Spirit, but to look for his lost asses (1 Sam. 9:3, 10:11, 31:4).

2. Only the man of prayer can worship God in spirit

and in truth. Others are like sensitive plants. When they are at worship they are affected by the teaching and presence of the Holy Spirit and seem to shrivel, bowing their heads to become serious for a while. But scarcely have they left the church when they perk up and brightly go on in their usual old way.

3. If we do not care for a tree or a shrub which bears good fruit or flowers it will degenerate and return to its wild state. If the believer neglects his spiritual life through lack of prayer he ceases to abide in me. His carelessness will make him fall from that state of blessedness and he will sink once again into his old sinful ways and be lost.

4. You may think, when you see a crane standing motionless on the side of a pond or lake that it is reflecting on the glory of God or the excellent quality of the water. But no such thing! He stands there motionless for hours waiting to catch sight of a fish or frog, and the moment he glimpses it he springs upon it and gulps it down. When they come to pray and meditate many people are just like that crane. They sit by the shore of God's boundless ocean and give little thought to his majesty and love, or to his divine nature, and his holiness which cleanses us from our sin and satisfies the hungry soul. Instead, their thoughts are wrapped up in how to get a specially desired object to indulge their worldly senses.

So they turn from the source of true peace, immersing themselves in the fading joys of this world which pass away and die with themselves.

5. Water and oil both come from the earth. They may seem to be alike but they are the exact

opposite, for one extinguishes fire and the other adds fuel to it. Now the world with its treasures, and the heart athirst for God, are both God's creations. But to try to satisfy the heart with the wealth, pride and honours of this world is like trying to put out a fire with petrol. The heart can only find rest and satisfaction in God who created it. The longing desire of which it is conscious (Ps. 42:1-2) is eased in God alone. So to anyone who comes to me I will give that living water to calm his troubled heart. He will never again be thirsty but there shall be in him a well of water springing up into eternal life (John 4:14).

6. Men try uselessly to find peace in the things of this world. Experience has clearly shown that this world does not give true peace and lasting satisfaction. People of this world are like the boy who peels off layer after layer of an onion trying to find something inside but finds nothing at all since an onion is only a collection of skins. And this world and everything to do with it turns out to be meaningless emptiness (Eccles. 12:8), until men discover the true fountain of peace and life (Isa. 55:1; Jer. 2:13; Rev. 22:17).

7. The world is like a mirage in which the seeker of truth hopes that he will find something to satisfy his thirsty spirit. But he meets nothing but disappointment and despair. The water of life is not to be found in man-made tanks or cracked cisterns. I am the source of living water. Those who come to me in prayer with a pure heart will find me and will be satisfied by my eternal life-giving water (John 4:10-13; Rev. 22:17).

8. A woman was travelling along a mountain track

carrying her child in her arms when the child saw some pretty flowers and leapt out of its mother's arms to touch the flowers. But he fell on a rock and died instantly. Now it is perfectly clear that the child's safety and its nourishment were to be found in its mother's bosom, not in the fascinating flowers, which ended up causing death. Yet that is how a believer behaves whose life is not a life of prayer. When he catches sight of the fleeting, fascinating pleasures of the world, he forgets my love and care, which are far greater than those of a mother; he forgets the spiritual milk which I provide for him; he leaps out of my arms and is lost.

9. The child can't feed on his mother's milk without some effort on his part. In the same way my children whom I carry in my bosom can only obtain the spiritual milk which is able to save their souls if they earnestly seek it and draw upon it. And just as the child does not need to be taught but knows instinctively how and where to obtain food, so those born of the Spirit know by a spiritual instinct how to pray. It is not worldly philosphy or wisdom that shows my children how to obtain the milk of eternal life, but the spirit of prayer.

10. I have infused man with a hunger and thirst for God, so that daily he may be reminded of his dependence on his Creator. He won't be able unthinkingly to regard himself as God because his needs will force him to realise that his life is bound up with the one who created him. So he will come to live in me and I in him, and in me alone he will find true happiness and joy.

DIALOGUE 3

1. To pray is to be, as it were, on terms of friendship with me. And by being in communion with me in this way and abiding in me, a person becomes like me. There is an insect which feeds upon and lives among the grass and green leaves and becomes like them in colour. There is also the polar bear which lives in the white snow and has the same snowy whiteness. The skin of the Bengal tiger is patterned like the reeds in which it lives. And those who live in communion with me through prayer take on my nature and with the saints and angels become like me, formed in my image.

2. I took Peter, James and John into close fellowship with me on the Mount and revealed something of my glory to them. There they also saw two of the saints – Moses and Elijah. It was only for a short while, but my disciples were so captivated by that brief glimpse of my heavenly glory that they wished to build three shelters and live there (Matt. 17:1–5). How much more wonderful will be the happiness that comes to those when they enter into their longed-for heaven with innumerable saints and angels and share with me my full glory which never ends nor changes (John 17:24; Jas. 1:17). The man of prayer will never be alone. He will live with me and my holy ones for ever (Matt. 28:20; Zech. 3:7–8).

3. It is no great thing to control and utilise the powers of nature, whether lightning, wind, energy, or wild animals. But it is true to say that it is essential to gain mastery over the world, Satan and the self with all its passions. That is a momentous

feat. It is only to those who live a life of prayer that I give the power to overcome all the might of the enemy (Luke 10:17, 20), so that even while they live in this world, they can abide with me in heavenly places (Eph. 2:6). Satan, then, being below and they above, he is never able to reach them. They live with me for ever in safety without a tremor of fear.

Although men have control over the powers of nature they are not able to travel as far as the man of prayer. Such a man who has mastered self and Satan can range at will through the everlasting heavens.

4. The man of prayer gathers happiness and value from all God's creation without harming it in any way just as the bee collects the sweet juice of the flowers and turns it into honey without injuring their colour or fragrance. And as bees gather honey from flowers in all sorts of different places and store it in the honeycomb, so the man of God gathers sweet thoughts and feelings from every part of creation. Then in communion with his Creator he stores the honey of truth in his heart, so that anywhere, at any time, in peace with God he can taste with delight the sweet honey of God.

5. Now is the time to live as the five wise virgins did (Matt. 25:1–13), and store in the vessels of your heart the oil of the Holy Spirit. Otherwise, like the five foolish girls, you will meet with nothing but grief and despair. Now, too, is the time to collect the manna for the true Sabbath, that is, for the reign of a thousand years of eternal rest, otherwise there will be nothing left for you but sorrow and suffering (Exod. 16:15, 27). Pray that you will be saved from being caught out during the bitter

distress of the last days, or on that great last
Sabbath. The opportunity you have now will never
come again (Matt. 24:20-1).

Just as the climate brings about changes in the
shape, colour and growth patterns of plants and
flowers, so those who maintain communion with
me grow and change spiritually. They are transformed into my own glorious and incorruptible
image, shedding their old nature.

6. With my finger I wrote upon the ground the
sinful state of each of those who, despite their own
inner vileness, had brought along the woman taken
in adultery for me to condemn - so that one by one
they left her and went away ashamed. With my
finger, too, I point out in secret to my servants their
wounds of sin. When they repent, with a touch of
the same finger I heal them. Just as a child grasps his
father's finger to help him walk along with him, so I
with my finger lead my children along the road
from this world to their home of eternal peace and
rest (John 14:2-3).

7. Often men pray to the Father in my name when
they are not abiding in me. They take my name into
their mouths and on their lips, but not into their
hearts and lives. That is why they do not receive
what they pray for. But when I abide in them and
they in me, then whatever they ask of the Father
they receive, for in that state of abiding they pray
under the direction of the Holy Spirit, and the Holy
Spirit shows men what will glorify the Father and is
best for themselves and others.

If they are not living with me, they will experience the answer that a bad son received from a
governor whom his father had served with courage

and distinction. When the son presented his request in his father's name and asked for some help with employment the governor pointed out his evil life and habits. 'Don't come crying to me in your father's name,' said the governor, 'but first act as he did. Don't merely pay lip service to his high qualities. Carry them out into your life and then your request will be granted.'

8. There is a great difference between the prayers of those who worship and praise me with their lips and those who do so from their hearts. For example, there was a true worshipper who constantly prayed for his enemy's eyes to be opened so that he might see and accept the truth. This enemy, a worshipper in name only, prayed in hate for my true worshipper to be struck blind. Finally the prayers of the true worshipper were answered by the loving will of God: the man who had been a hypocrite, a worshipper in name only, received spiritual sight and understanding. He became a true worshipper of God, a convinced believer and with a heart full of joy he became a sincere friend and lasting brother of my true believer.

9. Prayer makes things possible for men which they find otherwise impossible. My believers experience wonderful things in this life that are not only contrary to the rules and opinions of this world, but are thought to be altogether impossible. Scientists do not see that the God who created all things in order and set laws for them cannot be imprisoned behind the bars of his own laws.

The ways of the great law-giver are beyond man's understanding. His eternal will and purpose is the blessing and prosperity of all his creatures.

The reason the natural man cannot grasp this fact is because he does not belong to God – spiritual things are spiritually discerned (1 Cor. 2:14).

The greatest of all miracles is the new birth. To the believer who has experienced this miracle all miracles become possible. Now in very cold countries it is common to see a bridge made of water. When the surface of a river is frozen hard the water beneath still flows freely on and men cross over this icy bridge safely and easily. But, if people perspiring in the heat of the tropics heard you speaking of a bridge of water spanning a flowing river, they would tell you to stop talking rubbish. They would say such a thing was against the laws of nature. There is the same huge difference between those who have been born again and live by prayer and those who live worldly lives centred on material things. The latter are so utterly ignorant of the life of the soul that they consider it impossible, for they can only understand the material world they live in.

10. The man who desires to receive through prayer all the blessings of the spiritual life must believe and obey in total obedience. The man who came to me with a withered hand (Matt. 12:10–13) was cured because he instantly obeyed when I commanded him to stretch out his hand. But suppose he had not obeyed but questioned me with 'How can I do that? If I'd been able to I would not have needed to come to you, would I?' and, 'First heal my hand and then I'll stretch it out.' All these arguments would have seemed very proper and reasonable, but his hand would never have been healed.

The man who prays must be obedient and

believing. Stretch out to me your weak and withered hands and I will give you spiritual healing and life. I will grant all things according to a man's needs (Matt. 21:22).

5 SERVICE

DIALOGUE 1

The disciple:

Master, what is the true meaning of service? Do we serve the Creator and then his creatures for his sake? How can man, who is a mere worm, be of any use to God in the care of his large family? Does God need man's help to protect and preserve his creatures?

The Master:

1. Service means the activity of the spiritual life. It is man's spontaneous love offering to God. God, who is love, is ever active in the care of his creation. He desires that all his creatures, especially man formed in his own image, should not be idle. God does not need man's help to care for his creatures. They are created in such a way that they could not continue to exist without his help, and he has provided all they need to satisfy them.

When truly serving others the man who serves greatly benefits. This was your experience in Tibet. There you were, in fear of death and bitterly cold, when you saw someone lying buried in the snow, at the point of death. You went to him and lifted him upon your shoulders and carried him onwards. The effort you made produced heat in your body which passed into his and it saved both of you. In rescuing that stranger you saved your life. This is the true end of service. No one can live alone, deprived of the help of others. If anyone receives help and is unwilling to return it when he can, then such an ungrateful fellow has no right to expect help from anyone at all.

2. Man must use in God's service all the abilities and powers with which God has provided him, otherwise he will not receive God's help. As soon as man does his part, God will complete it. For example, when Lazarus had died, man's part was the removal of the stone from Lazarus' tomb. That was not a job that needed God's power. But when the people had rolled away the stone, then God acted. I, God, did what was beyond the powers and abilities of man: I gave life to the dead. But after that there was still work for man to do: Lazarus had to be freed from his grave-clothes (John 11:39–44).

So for those still dead in sin, it is the work of my disciples to roll away the gravestones – all those problems which hinder people and make believing difficult – but it is my work to give life. Often, too, some who have received spiritual life still remain locked up in their old habits and evil associations and then it is the work of my children to lead these into perfect freedom. To render such a service to each other means always being alert to me in heart and soul.

3. There was a king, who, when he was dying, spoke

to a faithful servant: 'It has been my practice to send you before me when I set out on a journey so that you can announce my coming and make preparations for my reception. I am going to the land of the dead. So go and inform them that I am about to join them.' At first the faithful servant did not understand what his lord meant. But as soon as he realised that he was meant to die and thus precede his master into the land of the dead, without a moment's hesitation the servant plunged a sword into his own heart. So he entered the land of the dead to await his lord.

I am the Lord of life, the King of kings (Rev. 19:16). It is the duty of my servants to carry the gospel to those who are dead in sin and be ready to give their lives for me. I came to earth for man's salvation and will come once again.

4. A rebellious son once left his father's house and joined a gang of thieves. In time he became as brazen and ruthless as the rest. The father called his servants and ordered them to go and tell his son that if he would repent and return home all would be forgiven, and his father would welcome him home again. But the servants refused to go. They were terrified of the wild country and fierce robbers. Then, the elder brother who loved the son as much as his father, set off to carry the message of forgiveness. But soon after he had entered the jungle the elder son was attacked by the thieves who mortally wounded him. When the younger brother realised it was his own brother whom his gang had injured, he was full of grief and remorse. The elder brother delivered the father's message of forgiveness and then he died, his purpose in life

completed and love's duty done. This sacrifice of the elder brother deeply impressed the rebellious son and he returned to his father, deeply sorry and determined to lead a new life from that day on.

Isn't it right that my sons should also be ready to sacrifice their lives for their brothers who have gone astray and been ruined in sin. They, too, must be willing to go out with the message of forgiveness just as I gave my life for the salvation of man.

5. My children are like salt in the world (Matt. 5:13). If the salt crystals are not dissolved they cannot give out their flavour. That's how it is with my children. They must be melted in the fire of love by the Holy Spirit and made into living sacrifices. Then they will be able to bring to souls in need the spiritual and heavenly life by which men may be saved. If they don't, they will be no better than Lot's wife who became a pillar of salt (Gen. 19:26). In Gethsemane (Luke 22:44), I was melted for your sakes, and on the cross I gave my life to save the lives of men for life must be paid for with life. So you are also called to give your lives to bring spiritual life to others and deliver them from death.

6. A certain murderer was sent into battle instead of being hanged. On the battlefield he fought with fearless courage and although he was severely wounded he returned to his country a conqueror. After the victory he was brought into the court again to be given his sentence. But the king cancelled his death sentence when he witnessed the wounds of battle on his body. Not only did he forgive his crime, but he rewarded him highly, raising him to a position of honour in his court. So those who fight on my side against Satan in the holy

war, and with courage and boldness to save their fellow men, will receive my reward. I will forgive their sins and receive them into the kingdom of God where I will crown them with honour and give them a kingdom (Jas. 5:20; Rev. 3:21).

7. The pipe that carries clean water is itself washed clean by the water it conveys. Those who in the power of the Holy Spirit, carry the water of life to others are themselves purified and become heirs of the kingdom of God.

8. The best way for the believer to make himself fit to receive the Holy Spirit and to embark upon service is to be obedient. When he hears the heavenly voice, he must immediately begin to serve, with all the ability that he has.

If one wants to become a good swimmer, it is not much use just listening to the theory of swimming. One must enter the water and strike out for oneself. It is only by constant practice, first in shallow water, then in deep water, that one can become proficient. So, in order to know how to save souls who are sinking in the dark waters of sin, the best way is to enter the only real bible college – that is, to enter into union with me (Acts 4:13).

9. Some hold back from my service because of their lack of ability. They fail to remember that my strength gives power in weakness (2 Cor. 12:9). Like invalids, they remain weak because they don't take proper exercise or do any work. Yet they have recovered from their disease and are eating nourishing food. Such believers need to trust me and set out to serve me by saving sinners from destruction.

DIALOGUE 2

1. Love is the touchstone by which truth is perceived. By it all men will know who are my disciples (John 13:35). The sword of justice is mine to bring truth out of love. Some people think that I intend to finish my work without showing any mercy, like Solomon (1 Kgs. 3:16–28). But, like Solomon, my purpose is to apply the touchstone of love in order to show that you are the children of that God of love who gave his life for you. So live in that love and serve one another. Even give up your lives in service for each other as I did for you. Then you shall live, as I am living (John 14:19).

2. If you are my disciples, then your service of love will bear much fruit (John 15:8). If men speak evil of you criticising you for your goodness, then pray for them. Instead of hitting back at them, let them taste the sweet fruit of your love.

Mischievous boys throw stones at juicy fruit on a tree. Without a murmur the tree drops its fruit on them. The tree cannot throw stones. It can only return what it has without complaint: the sweet fruit which God has given it. Don't be cast down by ill-treatment. When men fling abuse at you it is full proof that yours is a fruitful life. Though they may treat you in this way, driven from envy and spite, yet your heavenly Father is revealed and glorified. Don't imagine that God hungers after glory or that man can supply something lacking in his glory. Not at all! The purpose of God's love is to lift miserable man out of the sinful state into which he has fallen and to bear him upwards to his own glory. God does not give glory to himself but to man by cleansing and purifying him. In this the wonder and majesty of God's love is shown.

3. I will give glory to those in my service who have enabled others to turn from sin and find righteousness in me. They will receive such glory that will make them shine like stars, and when they have been made perfect in the kingdom of their Father, they will shine like the sun. The stars in the sky fade and disappear at the rising of the sun of righteousness. But my Father's wish is that his sons should be like himself, perfect and shining with everlasting glory, rejoicing for ever in his boundless, eternal love.

4. There are little creatures like the firefly which are far inferior to man, yet give flickering light in the world. And there are some small plants among the vegetation in the Himalayas that illumine the dark jungles with their faint phosphorescent glow. Some tiny fish that swim in the deep ocean give out a shimmering light which guides other fish and helps them escape from their enemies. So how much more ought my children to be lights in the world (Matt. 5:14). They must be completely willing to sacrifice themselves so that they may bring others into the way of truth, by their God-given light. Only then can those who are in darkness and prey to Satan's attacks be guided safely away.

5. If they do not use their heaven-sent powers in the service of God and his people, my servants are in danger of losing those heavenly gifts for ever. This has happened to certain fish in the deep, dark waters and it happens to some hermits in Tibet – they have both lived in darkness for so long that

they have entirely lost their sight. Similarly, the ostrich has lost the power of flight completely by not using its wings. Be careful, then, not to neglect whatever gifts or talents that have been entrusted to you. Make use of them that you may share in the bliss and glory of your Master (Matt. 25:14–30).

6. Sometimes, when there is a great act of service to be done which will bring salvation and blessing to many, I choose those who are of little value in the world's eyes. They make no boast of their own power or wisdom, but put their entire trust in me. What small ability they possess they account of no great value, but instead devote their entire selves to my purpose and work (1 Cor. 1:26–30).

An example of this can be seen when I fed five thousand men with five loaves and two fish. My disciples did not help me to perform this miracle. They were full of doubt and confused, and they wanted to send the huge crowd away. I chose instead a small boy whom I had cured of paralysis to be my servant (John 6:9). He was determined to follow me and to hear my words. His poor mother had wrapped up in his clothes some barley cakes and dried fish. It was enough for two or three days' journey. When my disciples asked about among the crowds for food, this faithful lad immediately brought all he had and offered it to the disciples. There were wealthier people there with wheaten cakes, but they were not prepared to give them up. It was the simple barley bread of this boy that brought about a banquet as the crowds were filled.

7. Many people remain dissatisfied and ungrateful no matter what blessings they receive or what miracles they see performed for their benefit. Such

folk can never be used to bless and serve others. They are like the man whom I healed after he had suffered from an incurable disease for thirty-eight years. Instead of being grateful to me and believing in me he did not even trouble to remember my name (John 5:12-13). The world can hope for no blessing from such people. It comes only from those like the poor widow, who are ready to give up all they have, even all their income (Luke 21:2-4).

8. If they wish to render me true service and perform their duty as it should be done, my servants must be ready to offer life itself. They should be like that faithful soldier who remained at his post in the bitter cold and falling snow till he froze to death. He stood like a statue and kept his place, while his fellow men went off to warm themselves by the fire. When their king came and saw his body fixed and faithful in death, he took off his crown and placed it for a while on the dead soldier saying, 'Such a faithful soldier and servant of the king is worthy of a crown of honour and glory. Would that he had lived to be made a ruler in my kingdom!'

So I require my servants to be utterly faithful in the task to which I have appointed them. To those who like that soldier finish their work with faith and courage, I will grant a never-fading crown in my eternal kingdom (2 Tim. 4:4-8).

9. Many people have wasted the precious time I give them for my work. Even now they have an opportunity to rouse themselves and make the best use of the time that remains.

Instead, they are like the hunter who wandered through the jungle and found some pretty stones by the edge of a stream. Not knowing their value he put them in his sling and shot at the birds in the trees by the water. One by one each stone fell into the water and was lost. There was one stone left when the hunter decided to go back to the city. As he wandered by the bazaar, holding the pretty stone in his hands, a jeweller saw it and offered him a thousand rupees for such a valuable diamond. When the hunter realised his mistake he was beside himself with sorrow. 'What a fool I am!' he cried. 'How stupid I am! I have shot the birds with diamonds not knowing what they were! Now they're lost in the river. And I've lost my chance to be a millionaire! Still – I've got one left, and that's something.'

Every day is like a precious diamond. Though many priceless days have been wasted in the pursuit of passing pleasure and are sunk for ever in the depths of the past, you can wake up to the value of what remains. Bring what you still have left and put it to its best use so that you may gather spiritual riches for yourself. Use your days in my service, for I give you life with all its priceless blessings. Use it to save others from sin and death and you will receive the eternal riches of my heavenly reward.

6 THE CROSS AND THE MYSTERY OF SUFFERING

DIALOGUE 1

The disciple:

What is the meaning and purpose of the cross? Why do pain and suffering exist in the world?

The Master:

1. The cross is heaven's key. At the moment of my baptism I took the cross upon my shoulders for the sake of sinners. Then heaven was opened. For thirty-three years I bore my cross and then died upon it and heaven which had been closed because of sin, was for ever opened to believers.

Now, as soon as believers take up their cross and follow me, they enter heaven through me (John 10:9). They begin to enjoy an unbounded bliss which the world cannot understand, for heaven stays shut up against unbelief. Unbelievers learn by experience that joy follows pain. But that kind of joy does not last. It is not the joy I give to my children. They have comfort in pain, and perfect peace and happiness while they are suffering. Those who joyfully take up my cross are borne up by it and when they at last enter heaven they are still supported by it.

2. Pain comes because of man's perverted and rebellious nature. Tropical heat is annoying and painful to those who live in cold lands, and so is the bitter cold to people in the tropics. Heat and cold depend on the earth's relation to the sun. So man can enter into a stage of agreement or disagreement with God by exercising his own free will. The laws of God are intended for the spiritual health and happiness of man. Opposition to them brings spiritual pain and suffering. God does not remove these states of opposition and rebellion, but uses them to make it quite obvious to man that this world was not created to be his home. Man lives in it as a foreigner in a strange land (2 Cor. 5:1-2, 6).

This world is a preparation for man's perfect, eternal home. The many repeated blows of suffering are intended to keep his spirit awake and alert. Otherwise man would become careless and fall away from the truth to share in the ruin of this unstable world. God's plan was for man to live in communion with his Creator, and after being set free from the suffering and misery of this passing world, to enter heaven in eternal peace and happiness.

3. Pain and suffering are bitter poisons. But the antidote to poison is sometimes poison itself. So pain and suffering can be used as bitter medicines to bring about the spiritual health and life of my believers. As soon as they enter into perfect health,

in heaven, there will be an end of all suffering. Their pain is no pleasure to me. I want only eternal health for my children (Lam. 3:31, 33).

4. After an earthquake, springs of pure water sometimes rise up in desert places. Then the arid wasteland is irrigated and becomes fruitful. Similarly, in some cases the shock of suffering opens up hidden springs of living water within a man's heart. In place of complaints and grumbles streams of gratitude and joy flow from him (Ps. 119:67, 71).

5. When a baby enters the world it is important for it to cry, so that its lungs expand and breathe in fresh air. Sometimes it is necessary to slap the baby to make it cry. That's how it is with my perfect love. I sometimes cause my children to cry out in pain so that their spiritual lungs can expand in the breath of prayer. So they receive spiritual refreshment and abide in eternal life.

6. A walnut's outer rind is bitter, but its inner kernel tastes good and is refreshing. In the same way, the cross does not look anything at all. But its inner nature and character are revealed to the cross-bearer. The believer finds in it the choicest food of the spiritual life.

7. When I was born on earth I bore the cruel cross for man's salvation, not just for the six hours of my crucifixion, or the three and a half years of my ministry, but for my entire life. I carried my cross for all the thirty-three and a half years of my life so that man might be delivered from the bitterness of death.

A man who is clean finds it most unpleasant to stay for even a few minutes in a filthy, unclean place! So it is for those who live in me; they find it distasteful to live amid evil. That is why some men of prayer abandon the world. They are so upset by the foulness of sin that they go to live as hermits in deserts and caves. If men, who are themselves wrongdoers, feel the pressure of sin so hard to bear that they cannot endure the company of their own kind and leave them, never wishing to return, think how extremely painful my cross must have been for me. Consider this: I, the fountain of holiness, had constantly to live my life among men made rotten with sin. It is beyond the powers of man's mind to appreciate this properly and really grasp hold of it. It is something even the angels desire to look into (1 Pet. 1:12). Before creation the angels knew that God is love. Yet they found it a most wonderful and amazing thing that the love of God should become incarnate and bear the cruel cross, in order that his creatures might be saved and enter eternal life.

8. And while they are in this life I share the cross of those who abide in me and I enter into their sufferings (Acts 9:4). Though they are creatures and I am their Creator yet I am the life and spirit of my children and they are my body. Just as the body and spirit, though separate entities, are so inter-mingled that if the body feels pain the spirit immediately becomes conscious of it. So I share every pain and grief of my children and bring relief just at the right moment.

9. Since I myself bore the cross I am able to deliver and keep in perfect safety all who are cross-bearers. Even when they walk through the fires of persecution, I am there. I was with the three men in Nebuchadnezzar's furnace. With all its raging heat it had no power to hurt them (Dan. 3:23–5; 1 Pet.

4:12–13). So those who by the baptism of the Holy Spirit have received the new life will never feel the fires of persecution. Nothing will hurt them for they live in me, in eternal peace and safety.

DIALOGUE 2

1. In the bitter cold of winter the trees stand bare of leaves. It seems as if their very lives have departed for ever. Yet in the spring they shoot new leaves and beautiful blossom, and the fruit begins to bud. So it was with me in my crucifixion and resurrection. And so it will be for my faithful cross-bearers (2 Cor. 4:8–11; 6:4–10). Though they seem crushed and dead beneath their cross they will produce the beautiful blossom and glorious fruit of eternal life which goes on for ever.
2. When a sweet tree is grafted on to a bitter one, both trees feel the knife and both suffer, in order that the bitter tree may bear sweet fruit. So, for man's evil nature, poisoned by sin, to become holy and spiritual, first of all I myself, and afterwards believers, had to suffer the agony of the cross, that believers might for ever bear good fruit. In their own suffering as they are grafted into me, the glorious love of God is revealed.
3. This world is a battlefield. Do not be surprised or distressed when you are persecuted and ill-treated. It will be a sad time for you when men of this world praise you (Luke 6:26)! When that happens you will

know that you have taken on the world's perverted ways and habits because it is totally against the grain for people of the world to praise my children! Light and darkness just cannot co-exist. If evil men act against their nature and, for the sake of appearances, decide to stop persecuting you, then you will suffer all the more for it – for their influence will enter your spiritual life and hinder your spiritual progress.

To trust the world or men of the world is to build your house on the sand for they are totally unstable. Today they will raise you up high, but tomorrow they will cast you down with such ferocity that nothing will be left of you. 'Hosanna! Hosanna!' they all cried when I went up to Jerusalem (Matt. 21:9). A few days later they changed their cry to 'Crucify him! Crucify him!' (Luke 23:21). When the world saw that my words and life were against their life of sin and self-seeking, then they sided against me.

4. If through some misunderstanding a few, or even all, the believers turn against you, hurt you, do not regard it as something unfortunate. If, by the guidance of the Holy Spirit, in all honesty and sincerity, you have obeyed and done your duty, then God himself and all the hosts of heaven will be on your side.

Do not let yourself get discouraged. The time will come when all your good intentions and purposes, all your unselfish love will be made known to the world. In everyone's presence God will honour you for your faithful service and hard work.

I renounced all things for man's salvation. And I myself was renounced by the world. Yet in the end I regained everything. So don't be alarmed if the world deserts you. It deserted God himself. In this way you are seen to be a true son of your heavenly Father.

5. Don't imagine that those who live in luxury, and are successful in worldly affairs, are all true worshippers of God. Very often the opposite is true. It is possible for sheep to wander away from the fold and from the shepherd and still find good pasturage, but the sheep are constantly in danger of being torn to pieces by wild beasts and this is how they will end up. But those who remain in the fold with the shepherd, stay under the shepherd's care. They may appear weak and feeble but they are free from danger. This then is the difference between believer and unbeliever.

6. At first the lives of the believer and the unbeliever look alike, but they gradually grow apart. When their ends come they are as different as the snake and the silkworm. The snake remains a snake no matter how often he casts his skin, but the silkworm changes into a new creature when it casts off its unsightly cocoon. It becomes a pretty moth that flies in the air. So the believer casts aside his old nature and takes flight into spiritual glory, for ever in heaven. But the sinner remains a sinner even in death.

Cramped within the cocoon, the silkworm struggles and strains as though bearing the cross. Yet this same strife and difficulty strengthens its wings and fits if for its future life. Similarly my children struggle and strain in their earthly nature, sighing with longing as they look forward to their release. But as they bear their crosses I give them

strength, and so they are made ready for eternal life
(Rom. 8:23).

In the middle of this spiritual warfare, just when
they are carrying their crosses, I bring my followers
a truly wonderful peace of heart so that their
courage does not falter. When my faithful disciple
was martyred for witnessing about me in his words
and actions, he was hung upside down on a tree. But
his peace of mind was so great that he was utterly
unconscious of his pain and disgrace. He turned to
his persecutors and said, 'I am not dismayed. Praise
God for his glorious cross.' He expected nothing
else in this topsyturvy world, where nothing is seen
straight. His enemies had turned him upside down
because they themselves had got everything the
wrong way up, but for God he was the right way up.
A slide put into a projector upside down reproduces
the picture correctly. The world may scoff at my
child hung upside down, but he is ever the rightside
up for me.

7. It may be the call of some to become martyrs for
me, but I also need witnesses who will daily offer
themselves as living sacrifices for the salvation of
others (1 Cor. 15:31). For some people death may
seem easy. It is harder to live for me, for a believer's
life is a daily dying to the self. Those who are ready
to lay down their lives for my sake in this will share
my glory. They will live with me for ever in the
fullness of joy.

8. If pain, suffering, sorrow, and grief rise like
clouds and overshadow your life for a time, hiding
the sun of righteousness from view, do not be
discouraged. These clouds of distress will descend
in showers of blessing on your head. In the end the

sun of righteousness will rise for ever to set no
more (John 16:20–2).

7 HEAVEN AND HELL

DIALOGUE 1

The disciple:

Master, what are heaven and hell and where are they?

The Master:

1. Heaven and hell are two opposite states in the spiritual realm. Their origins lie in the heart of man and their foundations are laid here in this world. Since man cannot see his own spirit he cannot see these two states of the soul. But he can experience them within him just as he experiences pain from a blow, or sweetness from eating cake. Wounds caused by a blow get more and more painful until finally they end in gangrene and death. On the other hand, when sugar is digested it gives the body energy. Similarly, pain resulting from a sinful act, or happiness from a good deed are to some extent felt immediately in this world, but their true effect – whether penalty or reward – are perceived in the realm of the Spirit and realised after death.

2. In this world man is never satisfied for long with one thing, but is constantly in search of a change of

circumstances or surroundings. This is a sure indication that the fleeting things of this world will never satisfy him. What he really wants is something that is stable and unchanging and satisfies all his tastes and desires. When he seeks and finds this reality in me the need for any further change ends; one does not grow weary of perfection for this is the single longing of the body and spirit. In all truth the one desire of the human soul is for true peace.

There are times when sudden unlooked-for sensations of pleasure or pain pierce a man's heart. They come unsought from the spiritual states of heaven or hell and may occur again and again. Slowly, according to the habit of the man's spiritual life, one becomes more frequent until, at last, by steadily preferring one over the other, the man makes his final choice. In this way the foundation of heaven or hell is built upon a man's heart while in this world. After death he enters into that state which in this life his desires or passions have prepared him for.

3. Some say that desire is the root of all pain and sorrow and so it is not right to desire happiness in heaven or in communion with God. They think that salvation comes from killing all desire. But to say this is silly. It is like telling a thirsty man to kill his thirst instead of giving him water to drink. Desire, like thirst, is part of life itself. To take away either without satisfying them is to destroy life, which is not salvation but death. Thirst implies a need for water; water is intended to remove thirst. So the existence of desire in the soul implies the existence of true happiness and peace. When the soul finds

the one that gave it that desire, it receives its greatest satisfaction; satisfaction greater than that which comes from quenching human thirst. This spiritual satisfaction of the soul's desire is heaven.

4. There are many in this world who die of thirst. They are like the man who could not quench his thirst, though he was surrounded by water, for the water was the salty sea-water. In the same way, in God's boundless waters of love yet in their disobedience and sin, they find God's fresh water of grace distasteful. So they perish from thirst. But for those who repent of their sin and turn to me, fountains of life-giving water gush up from the depths of my love. These men find in the God who loves them the satisfaction they seek and enduring peace. There they enter heaven.

5. Many are so ardently devoted to this world that they are pulled irresistibly down by the force of its gravity and finally slip into hell. Though they have my teaching and example set before them, by my children, they fall, like stones thrown upwards for a while and then drawn back down to the ground. Yet when a man turns his heart to me in true repentance I forgive him. With whips of love I cleanse the temple and make it fit for the eternal dwelling of the King of kings. This earthly life is such that the glory and pomp of kings are here today and gone tomorrow. But those who become sons in the kingdom of God possess glory and honour, thrones and crowns, and a kingdom in heaven that has no end.

6. Sinners steal other people's property to increase their own pleasure. So people lock up their homes when they go away. This will continue as long as

men's hearts are locked in sin against their Lord and Creator. When, however, the lock of the heart is opened to God who patiently stands knocking at its door (Rev. 3:20), then the heart's desires and longings are fulfilled and there will be no more need to lock up houses. Instead of stealing each other's goods and hurting each other, men will serve each other in love. For when men give God what is his due they share in his love, serving one another and seeking only what is good. In this way they will enter God's wonderful joy and peace: this is heaven. 7. Two thieves died, one on either side of me, when I gave my life for mankind. To all outward appearances, we were just three men suffering the same fate. Yet from the spiritual point of view our deaths were vastly different. I died to save sinners from hell and lead them into heaven. One thief shut his heart against me and died unrepentant. But the other opened his heart to me in true repentance. He died in communion with me and found life. That very day he entered into Paradise with me (Luke 23:43).

Paradise does not only exist beyond the grave. It begins in the hearts of men now, though it is hidden from the eyes of the world. One of my faithful martyrs suffered untold agony in persecution. But when he was dying he was so filled with the joy of heaven that he told his persecutors, 'If only I could open my heart to show you the wonderful peace I have, which the world can neither give nor take away! Then you would be convinced of its truth! But this is the hidden manna which it is impossible for you to see.' So after his death those foolish men tore out his heart hoping to find something precious there. They found nothing, of course. The reality of heaven is known only to those who accept me and find their joy in me.

8. Mary's womb, where I lived for some months, was not such a happy place as the heart of a believer. There I make my home for ever and turn it into heaven (Luke 11:27–8).

9. Many long for heaven yet miss it completely by their own stupidity. Once a poor beggar sat for twenty-one years on top of a hidden room full of treasure. He was so eaten up with the desire to be rich that he hoarded all the coppers he received. Yet he died in miserable poverty, quite unaware of the treasure he'd sat on for so long. My word is near to you in your mouth and in your heart (Deut. 30:14).

10. Those who don't know the spiritual life maintain that it is impossible to experience real peace and true joy in this grief-stricken world. But those who have experience of the spiritual life know that the hidden fire of the Holy Spirit glows within them. Just as you can sometimes find hot-water springs flowing in the middle of the ice-fields of the polar regions, so in the middle of this cold, sorrowful world there are warm streams of heavenly peace flowing in the hearts of believers.

11. God has created all men in his own form and likeness. They are all made of the same flesh and blood. Yet they are different in character, temperament and abilities. If all the flowers in the world looked the same and smelled the same the countryside would lose its charm. The sun's rays pass through coloured glass and the colours stay the same as the sunlight draws out their varied beauty and charm. In the same way the sun of

righteousness displays his glory and love through
the God-given virtues of saints. They are the ones
who live in me and they will have joy for evermore.

DIALOGUE 2

The disciple:

*Master, some people say that the comfort and joy that believers
experience are merely the consequence of their own thoughts and
ideas. Is this true?*

The Master:

1. That comfort and lasting peace within believers
comes from my presence in their hearts and from
the Holy Spirit who gives them life. Those who
attribute this spiritual joy to subjective thinking are
like the foolish blind man sitting in the winter
sunshine to warm himself. When people asked him
what he thought of the warm sun's rays, he firmly
denied such a thing as a sun.

'This warmth,' he said, 'comes from within my
own body. It is nothing more than the powerful
heat generated by my own thoughts. Don't talk
nonsense about this big ball of fire hanging up in
the sky.'

So watch out! 'See to it that no one takes you
captive through hollow and deceptive philosophy,

which depends on human tradition and the basic principles of this world rather than on Christ' (Col. 2:8).

2. If true happiness depended on the thoughts of · man, then all philosophers and deep thinkers would overflow with it. But apart from those who believe in me, men who are worldly-wise are totally unable to achieve happiness. All they can produce is a fleeting intellectual pleasure which they find in following certain rules and understanding of their own.

One of the basic properties of charcoal is that it will burn, but without oxygen it won't catch alight. That is how it is with man. I have built into him an innate ability to be filled with heavenly joy and to need life. But unless the oxygen of the Holy Spirit enters man's soul, he will remain as dark as coal, never able to come alight with true and lasting peace.

3. This ability of man's mind and heart is also like the strings of a violin. When the strings are tightened and harmonised the bow produces the most charming music, otherwise the touch of the bow will produce discords. Again, the sweet sounds that come when the strings are in tune, depend on the air to produce and carry them to the listening ear. In the same way, to create beautiful harmonies with thoughts and imaginations of men, the breath of the Holy Spirit is vital. In the presence of the Spirit, heavenly tunes and joyful melodies are created in men's hearts, both in this life and in the next.

DIALOGUE 3

The disciple:

Master, sometimes I am aware that my peace and happiness have gone. Is this because of hidden sin or some other reason unknown to me?

The Master:

1. Yes, this is sometimes the result of disobedience. But occasionally I appear to leave my children lonely and restless for a while because then I am able to reveal to them what they are really like: utterly weak and nothing but dry bones apart from me (Ezek. 37:1-14). They will think that they do not need me if they live in a constant state of ease and rest, and then, in their pride, they will presume that they are as good as God and so fall, and end up being punished in hell (1 Tim. 3:6; Jude 6; Isa. 14:12-17). So in this way I teach my children and bring them up, to walk humbly with me their Creator, that they will enter eternal joy in heaven.

2. At times when I enter into my children and fill them with the fullness of the Spirit they overflow with such divine happiness that they are not able to endure the glory and blessing that I bring to them, and they feel faint, or even lose consciousness. This is because flesh and blood cannot inherit the kingdom of God; neither can earthly things the eternal. First men must be freed from the power of this empty world and lifted to my glory (1 Cor.

15:50, 53; Rom. 8:19–22). Then my will shall be done on earth as it is in heaven. Then pain and suffering, sorrow and grief, evil and death shall be removed for ever. All my children shall enter the kingdom of my Father and there in the joy of the Holy Spirit they shall reign for ever and ever (Rom. 14:17; Rev. 21:4; 22:5).

8 A PRAYER

Dear Master,
My heart overflows with gratitude and praise from your many blessings and gifts to me. But the praise of my heart and lips are not enough for me to show you my devotion; I must prove this by my action and service.

I thank you and praise you for bringing me, worthless as I am, out of death into life. You have made me able to rejoice in your fellowship and love.

I know nothing of myself or my needs, but you, Father, know everything about your creatures. Nor can I love myself as you love me. To love myself in the right way, I must, with all my heart, mind and soul, love the boundless love which made me. You are that love. You gave me only one heart so that I might concentrate on you alone, my Creator God.

Master, to sit down at your feet is far better than to sit on the mightiest throne of this world. By your feet I am enthroned for ever in the eternal kingdom. So now, on the altar of those sacred feet, I offer myself as a living sacrifice. By your grace accept me and use me in your service wherever and however you please.

You are mine and I belong to you. From a handful of dust you formed me in your own image, and gave me the right to be called a son of God.

All honour, glory, praise and thanksgiving be to you, my Lord, for ever and ever. Amen.

THE LITTLE FLOWERS OF ST FRANCIS

Translated by E M Blaiklock and A C Keys

The Acts of Saint Francis and his Companions contains 77 brief chapters or 'acts', 54 of which are better known as *The Little Flowers of Saint Francis*. This masterly new translation of the unabridged text by Professors Blaiklock and Keys will be greatly appreciated by scholar and layman alike.

This medieval Italian manuscript is one of the most cherished texts of Western spirituality and introduces the modern reader to the sayings and deeds of a remarkable man and his companions. Their spirit of integrity, love and devotion shines through, and the many stories, aphorisms, teachings and miracles will astound and enchant the reader. The thought and radical example of Saint Francis has inspired countless Christians throughout the ages, and will continue to challenge many today.

THE CLOUD OF UNKNOWING

Edited by Halcyon Backhouse

The latter half of the fourteenth century was a turbulent period: the great plague had just swept through England decimating its population; the hundred years war with France was drawing to its bitter end; social unrest was endemic; the church was further and further divorced from its people. Against this background *The Cloud of Unknowing* was written. Its powerful message of God's unconditional love in the face of despair is as relevant today as it was 500 years ago.

The unknown author acknowledges that often at the height of the Christian's effort to love and know God he is faced with silence, an impenetrable wall – the dark cloud of unknowing. He assures the reader that perseverance and abandonment to God's boundless love will enable him to experience a fuller, deeper spiritual life, based on true love and devotion. He calls us to a deeper life in the Spirit.

THE CONFESSIONS OF SAINT AUGUSTINE

New translation with introduction by E M Blaiklock

Augustine towered as a Christian leader in his own age, and is probably the greatest of the fathers of the Church. The *Confessions* has become a classic of all time, revealing an individual in the joys and agonies of life lived to the full in the search of truth. His confession of sin becomes a confession of Christ as Saviour, and a shining testimony to the grace of God.